W9-BZU-102

INSECTS: SIX-LEGGED NIGHTMARES

JAPANESE GIANT HORNETS HORRIFY!

BY JILL KEPPELER

Gareth Stevens
PUBLISHING

Please visit our website, www.garethstevens.com. For a free color catalog of all our high-quality books, call toll free 1-800-542-2595 or fax 1-877-542-2596.

Cataloging-in-Publication Data

Names: Keppeler, Jill.
Title: Japanese giant hornets horrify! / Jill Keppeler.
Description: New York : Gareth Stevens Publishing, 2018. | Series: Insects: six-legged nightmares | Includes index.
Identifiers: ISBN 9781538212639 (pbk.) | ISBN 9781538212653 (library bound) | ISBN 9781538212646 (6 pack)
Subjects: LCSH: Hornets–Juvenile literature.
Classification: LCC QL568.V5 K47 2018 | DDC 595.79'8–dc23

First Edition

Published in 2018 by
Gareth Stevens Publishing
111 East 14th Street, Suite 349
New York, NY 10003

Designer: Laura Bowen
Editor: Ryan Nagelhout/Kate Mikoley

Photo credits: Cover, pp. 1 (Japanese giant hornet), 11 (both) Alastair Macewen/Oxford Scientific/Getty Images; cover, pp. 1–24 (background) Fantom666/Shutterstock.com; cover, pp. 1–24 (black splatter) Miloje/Shutterstock.com; cover, pp. 1–24 (web) Ramona Kaulitzki/Shutterstock.com; pp. 4–24 (text boxes) Tueris/Shutterstock.com; p. 5 (main) Tarabagani/Wikimedia Commons; p. 5 (inset) colin robert varndell/Shutterstock.com; p. 7 David Carillet/Shutterstock.com; p. 9 (map) illpos/Shutterstock.com; p. 9 (field) Blanscape/Shutterstock.com; p. 9 (city) Sean Pavone/Shutterstock.com; pp. 13, 19 Alpsdake/Wikimedia Commons; p. 15 Takahashi/Wikimedia Commons; p. 17 feathercollector/Shutterstock.com; p. 21 Photography by Shin. T/Moment/Getty Images.

Printed in the United States of America

CPSIA compliance information: Batch #CW18GS: For further information contact Gareth Stevens, New York, New York at 1-800-542-2595.

CONTENTS

Words in the glossary appear in **bold** type the first time they are used in the text.

HUGE, HORRIBLE HORNETS

We share Earth with about 1 million species, or kinds, of **insects**. These sometimes creepy—often crawly—creatures fly, hide, and rush all around us. Most insects are so small that humans usually don't fear them. However, some insects can really pack a punch!

The Japanese giant hornet is one of the biggest types of hornets alive today. These big bugs can destroy a hive of honeybees in hours. They can even kill humans with the deadly **venom** in their sting.

TERRIFYING TRUTHS

A hornet is a large type of wasp. There are about 20 different kinds of hornets.

Japanese giant hornets don't live in the United States. Only one kind of hornet, the European hornet, can be found here.

European hornet

Japanese giant hornet

BIG, BAD BUGS

Japanese giant hornets are a type of Asian giant hornet. These big bugs are usually about 1.4 inches (3.5 cm) long, and the queen hornets can be even bigger! Their wings can stretch up to 2.8 inches (7.1 cm) across.

Like other wasps, this kind of hornet has antennae, two sets of eyes, and a smooth body. The abdomen, or rear part of their body, is pointed. It's connected to the thorax, or middle part, by a pinched-in area called the petiole.

TERRIFYING TRUTHS

A Japanese giant hornet's stinger can be 0.25 inch (0.6 cm) long. However, only female wasps can sting.

PARTS OF A JAPANESE GIANT HORNET

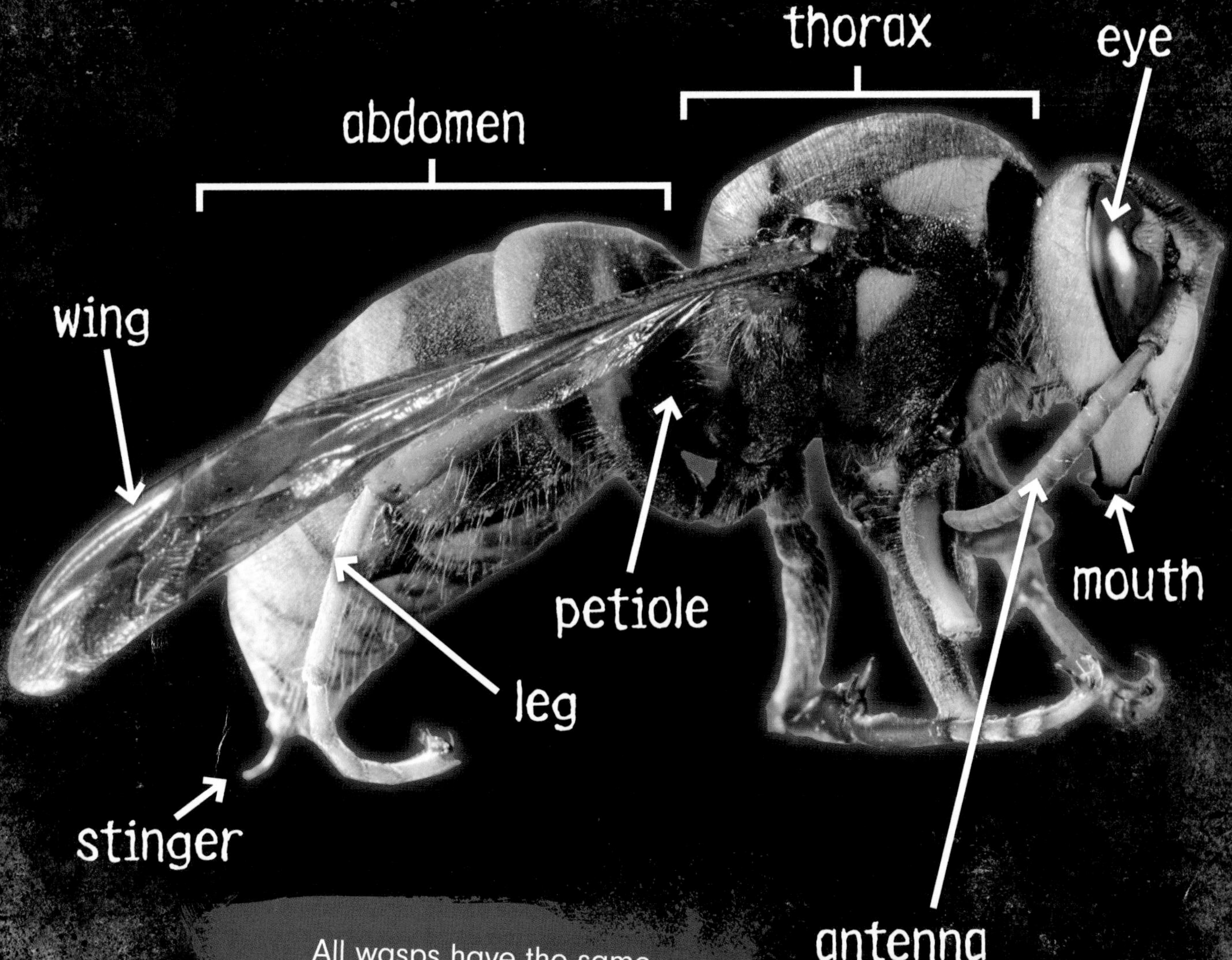

thorax

eye

abdomen

wing

petiole

mouth

leg

stinger

antenna

All wasps have the same basic parts. The parts are just bigger in Asian giant hornets!

HOME SWEET HORNET

Asian giant hornets live throughout Asia, but Japanese giant hornets live, of course, on the islands of Japan. Many live in the country, in the forests and mountains, but they've spread to the cities as well.

Japanese giant hornets build huge nests that can weigh more than 20 pounds (9.1 kg). These nests can often be found in holes in the ground, but sometimes the hornets build them in trees. The nests are made of a paperlike matter the wasps create from wood.

TERRIFYING TRUTHS

Japanese giant hornets often build their nests near areas where people farm. Farmers have to watch where they step!

WHERE THE JAPANESE GIANT HORNET LIVES

Hokkaido

Pacific Ocean

JAPAN

Honshu

Honshu countryside

Tokyo

Tokyo

Shikoku

Kyushu

Japanese giant hornets live throughout Japan. Many live on the island of Honshu, Japan's biggest island.

HONEYBEE HORROR

The Japanese giant hornet is a carnivore. That means it eats other animals. It eats many kinds of insects, including other hornets, but its favorite **prey** is the European honeybee.

If a hornet finds a hive of honeybees, it will mark the area with a **chemical** called a pheromone (FEHR-uh-mohn). This helps other hornets find the hive. The hornets will attack the bees, biting off their heads and cutting them to pieces with their sharp **jaws**. Then they'll take the bees' larvae and honey.

TERRIFYING TRUTHS

One Japanese giant hornet can kill up to 40 European honeybees a minute. Several hornets can kill 30,000 bees in 3 hours!

attacking the hive

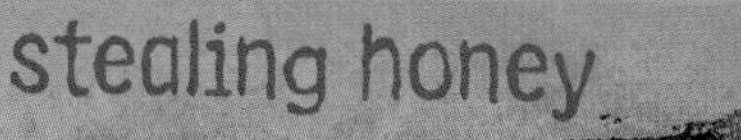
stealing honey

People brought the European honeybee to Japan because it makes more honey than the Japanese honeybee. However, the European honeybee has no **defense** against the Japanese giant hornet.

MMM, HORNET SPIT

The hornets carry the honeybee larvae back to their nest. There, they'll chew them into a paste that they feed to their own larvae.

The larvae, in turn, make a liquid in their spit that the adult hornets drink. This liquid is called vespa amino acid mixture, or VAAM. It's like an **energy** drink for hornets! One company has even made a drink for people using the same kinds of things found in VAAM. Would you drink hornet spit?

TERRIFYING TRUTHS

Japanese giant hornets sleep for about 6 months of the year. The queens wake in the spring and start laying thousands of eggs. These hatch into larvae in a week.

Japanese runner Naoko Takahashi, who won a gold medal at the 2000 Summer Olympics in Sydney, Australia, said the VAAM energy drink helped her win.

BEES FIGHT BACK!

While the European honeybee has no way to defend against Japanese giant hornets, Japanese honeybees have an unusual way to fight back. They can hug a hornet to death!

If a hornet scout finds a beehive, the Japanese honeybees will surround and squash the hornet until the bigger creature can't move. Then they'll make many small, fast movements, which makes the heat inside the bee ball rise. It gets so hot that the hornet dies!

TERRIFYING TRUTHS

Inside a hornet-killing bee ball, it can get up to 116°F (47°C).

Japanese honeybees have to be very careful to get the heat in their bee ball just right to kill a hornet, but not the bees themselves. Scientists are studying how they do this.

HORNETS VS. PEOPLE

Japanese giant hornets can be very dangerous to people. Humans aren't their usual prey, but they'll attack if people bother their nests. They don't lose their stinger after attacking, so they can sting over and over again.

The venom used by Japanese giant hornets is strong. It can disintegrate, or break down, human flesh! It can shut down people's kidneys or stop their heart if they're stung enough times. Special chemicals in the venom make it hurt even more.

TERRIFYING TRUTHS

Japanese giant hornets can fly up to 25 miles (40 km) an hour. The average person can't run nearly that fast!

These hornets are most active in August. People in Japan know to be very careful during this time.

INVASION OF THE HORNETS

In Japan and other Asian countries, dozens of people die each year after being stung by giant hornets. Most of these deaths are because of an allergy to the hornets' venom. This means their bodies attack themselves because of it.

In 2013, 42 people in China died from giant hornet stings in just a few months. The hornet attacks injured more than 1,600 people and more than 200 had to be treated in hospitals. The hornets attacked farmworkers and even **invaded** schools!

TERRIFYING TRUTHS

If you're ever attacked by Japanese giant hornets, don't run. They're more likely to attack if you do! Just walk away.

The hornet problem in one area of China was so bad in 2013 that officials warned people to wear long sleeves when they went outside.

PART OF THEIR WORLD

Japanese giant hornets seem very scary. However, they're an important part of their **ecosystem**. They help keep pests under control by eating other insects, such as caterpillars, that can harm crops.

As cities grow and people spread out, they may move into more areas where hornets live. People and giant hornets have to live with each other. These big, bad bugs don't want to hurt humans. If we're careful and leave them alone, they'll leave us alone, too!

TERRIFYING TRUTHS

Some people in Japan and other parts of Asia eat Japanese giant hornets. Would you try this special dish?

If you see a hornet of any kind, it's best to just leave it alone!

GLOSSARY

chemical: matter that can be mixed with other matter to cause changes

defense: a way of guarding against an enemy

ecosystem: all the living things in an area

energy: power used to do work

hatch: to break open or come out of

insect: a small, often winged, animal with six legs and three main body parts

invade: to enter a place to take it over

jaws: the walls of the mouth

prey: an animal that is hunted by other animals for food

venom: something an animal makes in its body that can harm other animals

FOR MORE INFORMATION

BOOKS

Klepeis, Alicia. *Praying Mantis vs. Giant Hornet: Battle of the Powerful Predators*. North Mankato, MN: Capstone Press, 2016.

Murawski, Darlyne, and Nancy Honovich. *Ultimate Bugopedia: The Most Complete Bug Reference Ever*. Washington, DC: National Geographic, 2013.

Rake, Matthew. *Creepy, Crawly Creatures*. Minneapolis, MN: Hungry Tomato, 2016.

WEBSITES

Asian Giant Hornet
https://a-z-animals.com/animals/asian-giant-hornet/
This website gives more information about the Asian giant hornet, including how it behaves and how it eats.

Attack of the Japanese Giant Hornets
www.natgeotv.com/uk/nature-uncut/videos/attack-of-the-japanese-giant-hornets
Watch a group of Japanese giant hornets attack a hive of honeybees and learn about how the attack was filmed.

Where Do Japanese Giant Hornets Live?
animals.mom.me/japanese-giant-hornets-live-11163.html
Learn more about where these big, bad hornets live—and how to stay away from them!

INDEX